How to be the Best Home Buyer: A Stress-free Guide to Buying a Home in Nashville

Amy Robinson

ISBN: 1546627782
ISBN-13: 978-1546627784

DEDICATION

This book is dedicated to my family who have always encouraged me in my quest to be the best real estate agent possible. Especially to my husband, Jake, for putting up with me working all hours of the day and night. I love you!

CONTENTS

ACKNOWLEDGMENTS

To all my vendor partners, especially John Barnes and Wanda Wilson, two of the best lenders I know, Aaron Schroer, a rock star inspector who has mentored my husband, "Warranty" Wes Poole, for your knowledge, and Doug Soehner, my Comcast man, for always being available to help my clients. This book would not have been possible without your support. To all the agents who have helped to inspire me along the way, Joey, Steve, Sarah, Shannon, and The Parks Crew in Mt. Juliet you guys have made me a better agent. Without your knowledge and advice, I would be lost, THANK YOU!

WHY DO YOU WANT TO BUY A HOME?

Most people start the home-buying process by searching websites or driving around neighborhoods they like. While this can help determine what styles or areas you like, it does not address the bigger question of WHY? Why do you want to buy a home?

Figuring out your WHY is the first and most crucial step in the home-buying process. For some buyers, it is as simple as getting a new job and the need to relocate closer to work. Other buyers may want to be in a better school district because they want to start a family. For many, the need to own a home comes from a deep-down desire to have the financial freedom one day that we all seek. Regardless of your WHY, now is the time to pinpoint it.

You may think you already know your reasoning, but I suggest you take it one step further and dig deeper. Take out a sheet of paper and write down why you want to own a home. Look at what you've written down and ask yourself why this is important. Once you have answered that question, ask yourself again why this is important and how it will change your life. Continue asking yourself this question till you have drilled down exactly what your goal is and be specific. Be sure and write down your answers.

<u>Here is an example:</u>

Why do I want to own a home?

Sick of renting

Why is it important I stop renting?

Throwing money away, too expensive

Why is it important I stop wasting money?

I want to save money and pay off debt

How would paying off debt and saving money change my life?

I would be less stressed and able to spend less time working, which gives me more time to spend with my family

<u>I WANT TO BUY A HOME, SO I CAN BE LESS FINANCIALLY STRESSED AND SPEND MORE TIME WITH MY FAMILY.</u>

Some people may be able to figure their true motivations out quickly, while others may find this more difficult. The key is to be honest and remember knowing your goals is the first step to achieving them! Now that you know why you want to buy a home, you can use this insight to help with all future decisions you will need to make in this process.

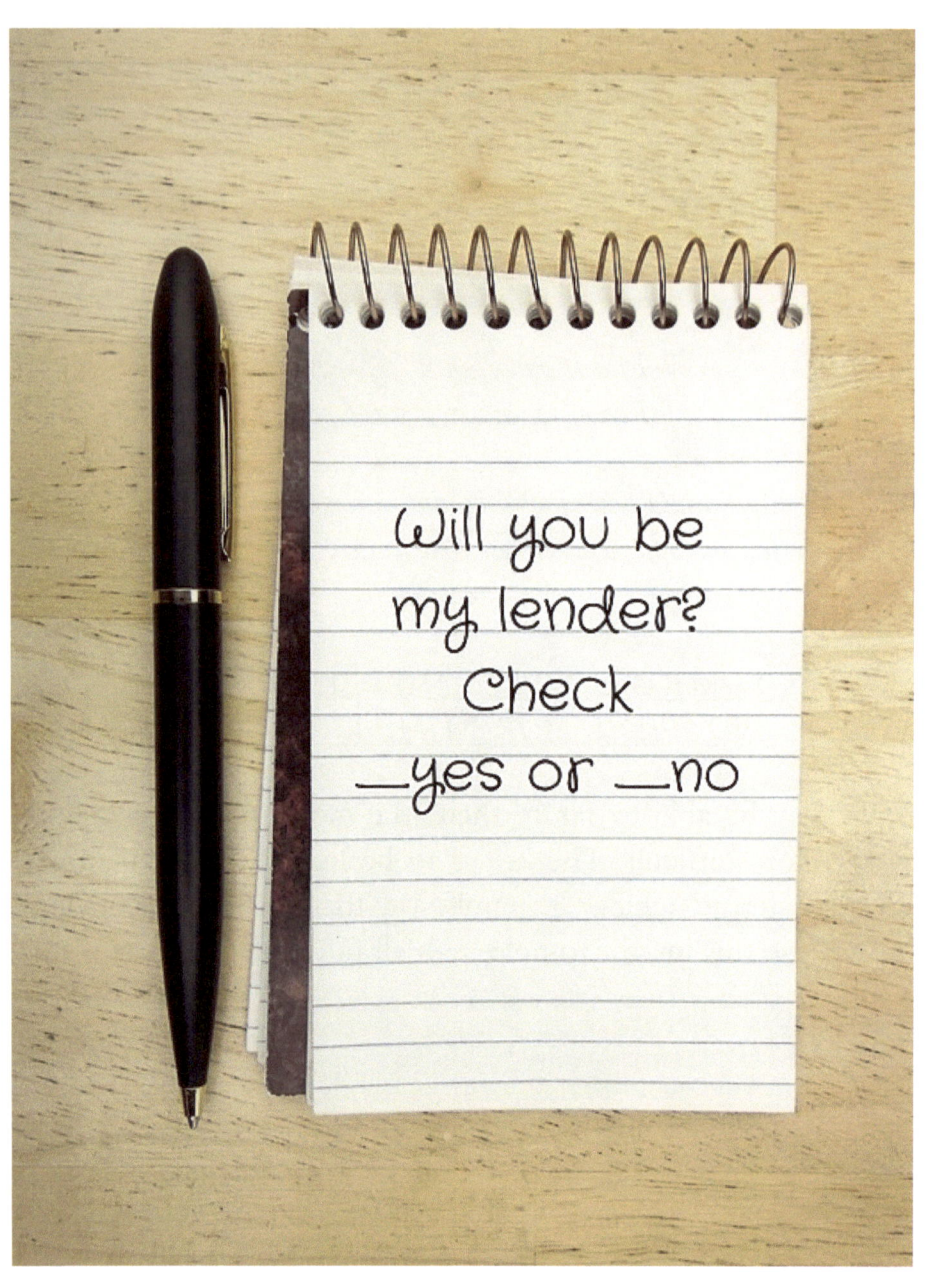

2

SHOP YOUR LENDERS

Shopping for a mortgage lender is an important step in the home-buying process. Many do not realize how many different options are truly available to the average consumer. Choosing the right lender is just as important as choosing the right house. For most people, this is the biggest financial investment you will ever make, so having the right person to guide you through the process is key.

There are national banks like Regions, Bank of America and Wells Fargo who offer mortgage lending options. These banks do tend to have decent rates, but often take longer than the average 30-45 days to close. Typically, the big banks have underwriting done at their home offices, which means not locally. In my experience, the buyer feels more like a loan number than a person.

The most popular choice in this area for lending would be a community bank or local lender. We have so many amazing options in Middle Tennessee you can really shop around and find the person you want to work with. A couple examples of great local lenders are Franklin Synergy and Southern Bank of Tennessee. Both are growing extensively in this market and have extremely competitive rates, but more importantly they will do whatever it takes to get you closed on time.

Regardless of the lender you choose, they will want some general information on an application to get you a pre-approval. It is true they will want to run your credit, but do not worry about a big drop in your score. Typically, when shopping for a mortgage, multiple credit inquiries from different lenders in a short period of time will not have a negative effect. The credit checks are treated as a single inquiry with little impact on your score and they give lenders the information needed to give you an accurate quote.

If you want to prevent all credit checks, you can seek pre-qualification instead. A pre-qualification uses information you provide and does not go into a detailed credit report to verify what you provided. I always recommend a pre-approval over pre-qualification if you are serious about buying in the next 3 months. A pre-approval gives you more confidence knowing you can get a loan compared to a pre-qualification which tells you what you might get approved for.

Once your lender has all the information needed to provide a quote, you will want to ask for a rate sheet. This will allow you to see upfront what they charge and what rate to expect. The rate sheet is a good way to compare lenders to one another and decide who is offering the best options for you. Keep in mind if you meet a loan officer you want to use but their rate is not as good as others, you can ask them to lower it. This is a negotiation, so do not be afraid to ask for help on closing costs or rate. Many lenders are willing to help a qualified buyer save money where they can if you decide to work with them.

Something else to remember while looking for the right lender is personality. Buying a home can be a stressful process, especially if you do not like the person trying to help you. So, if for whatever reason you do not click personally with them, do not use them! I have seen buyers miserable because they just went with the first person to give them an approval. Find a lender you feel confident in and that you can trust, it will make buying a home much more enjoyable.

Here is a list of some sample questions you may want to ask when interviewing a lender:

What will my closing costs be?
When will my rate be locked and what will it cost me?
How quickly can you close a loan?
What type of loan is best for me and why?
How much can I get approved for?
Is this the best rate you offer?
Do you work weekends?
Do you have a team, or will you be my primary point of contact?
How often will I get updates on my loan status?

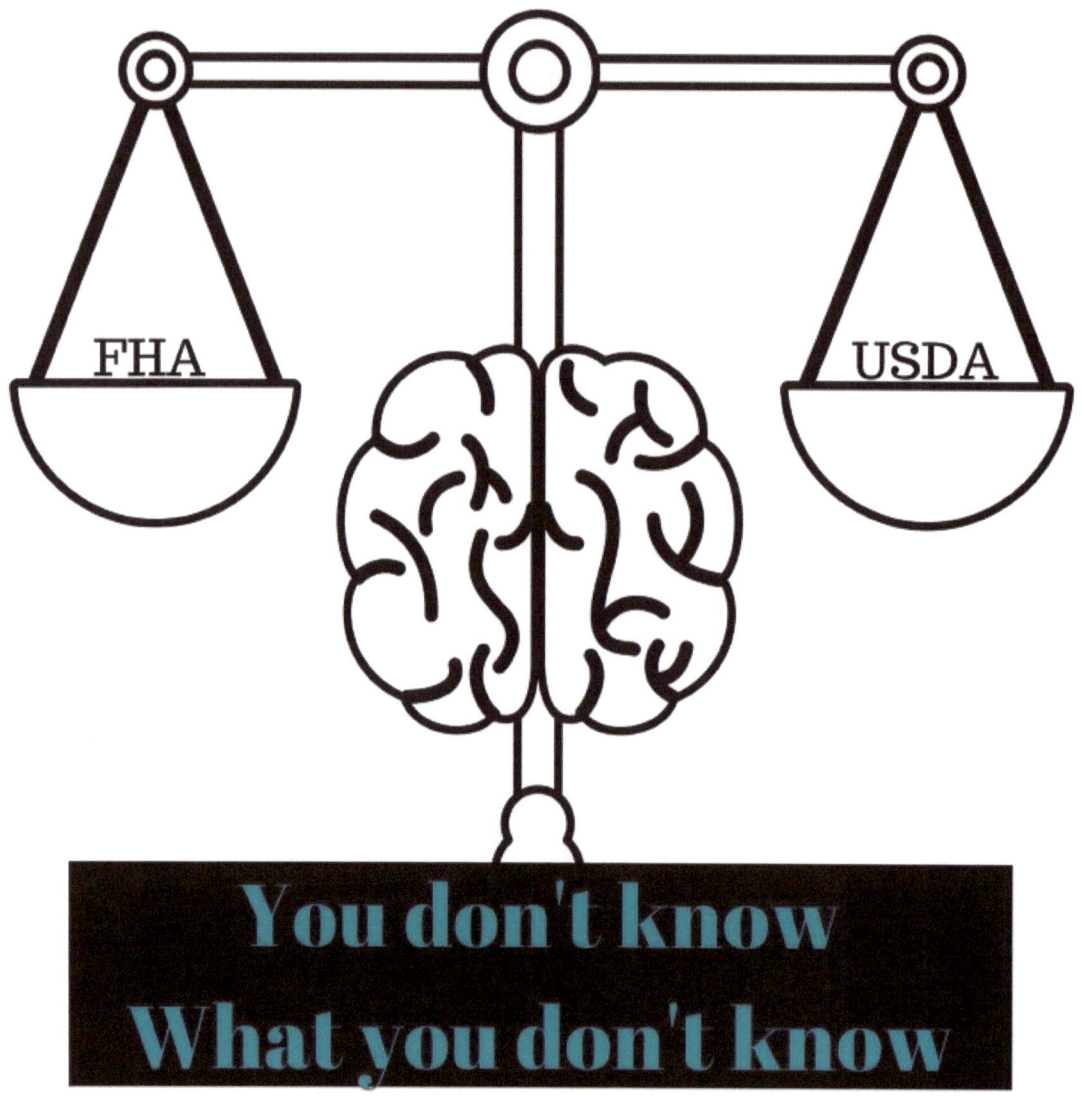

3

LOOK AT ALL LOAN OPTIONS

I have spoken to countless individuals who believe they need 20% in cash for a down payment before they can even think about buying. This is just not the case anymore. It is true a significant down payment can lower your monthly payment and prevent you from paying private mortgage insurance (PMI), but it is not a requirement.

These days, the amount of different loan options available is much wider than just a conventional 30-year mortgage with 20% down. Therefore, it is important you ask about all the options to find the one that fits your needs best. For example, first time homeowners can qualify for options current homeowners cannot. On the flip side, if you currently own a home, you may want to discuss loan options that allow you to use the equity you already have to qualify.

There are a few general rules of thumb lenders consider regardless of the loan type. Before you buy a home, you must prove you can afford it, typically by supplying pay stubs or tax returns. Generally, your mortgage payment (including principal, interest, taxes, and insurance or PITI) cannot be greater than 28% of your total monthly income. Also, if you add your total installment debt (e.g. car payments) to that payment, the total should not be greater than 38% of your monthly income. Credit score is another important factor used to determine what you will qualify for. A score above 700 is preferred, but lenders can work with scores as low as 620 in some instances.

Note on credit scores: Do not get discouraged if your score is lower than you expect. Many lenders offer services to help improve your score and it happens quicker than you would think. I have seen many instances where a client has a low score due to errors that can be easily corrected by the credit bureaus. With a little advice from an expert, your score could jump as much as 50 points in a few months.

The last thing to consider regardless of the type of loan is closing costs. These fees can range anywhere from 2-5% of the loan amount. They include items such as origination fees, appraisal, title fees, document preparation, etc. Also, pre-paid fees are often lumped into closing costs and include taxes, insurance, HOA fees, inspections, etc. So even if you get a 100% loan, you will still have out-of-pocket expenses of some sort. Since these fees do vary, it is important you discuss this with your lender and get an estimate of cost upfront in writing.

Here are a few of the popular loan options available in the Nashville area currently:

FHA: This is a popular option for first-time buyers who do not have a huge amount in savings for a down payment. Currently, you can qualify for as little as 3.5% down with an FHA loan. Closing costs do tend to be a little higher on these loans and you are required to pay mortgage insurance (MIP). MIP is currently 0.85% of the loan amount annually and paid for the life of the loan. FHA loans can be attractive if your credit score needs improvement, some lenders can work with buyers who have scores as low as 620. Since these loans are backed by the government, there are more hoops to jump through and the condition of the home plays a role in the approval process. If you are looking for a fixer upper, this might not be your best option.

VA: Offered to active duty and veterans of the military, this loan option is backed by the US government. If you qualify, this loan offers buyers no down payment and no mortgage insurance. There is still a small fee involved, but it is a great option for people who served our country to own a home.

Conventional: Traditionally, the most commonly used loan, conventional loans vary from 3%-20% down with private mortgage insurance. With a conventional loan, if you have 20% or more in down payment, no PMI is required. Also, on the loans with less than 20% down, the PMI is cancelable if your equity reaches greater than 20% (this happens when a home's value increases and/or the loan is paid down). PMI tends to be less expensive than the MIP required on government-backed loans. Most lenders do want to see a credit score of at least 680 to qualify for a conventional loan.

USDA/THDA: A great option for people in Middle Tennessee who may not want to live in the city is USDA. This loan option offers 100% financing in specific rural areas if you meet the income requirements. The income requirements vary depending on the location of the home you want to buy. For example, currently, a 2-person household in Wilson County who makes $50,000 in annual gross income would qualify for a loan with no down payment required. Another benefit of USDA is the lack of mortgage insurance. You are required to pay an upfront fee, but it is less than FHA or Conventional mortgage insurance fees. If you are interested in a rural area and your income qualifies, this is a good option for you to discuss with your lender.

Those are only a few of the options available, of course, your lender will provide details as to which may fit your needs best. The primary things to consider are: Down payment, mortgage insurance, upfront fees, term, and income requirements. There are also grant programs available to assist with down payments for those who qualify, so be sure and ask your lender for more information on any available when you apply.

APPROVAL

Does Not Equal

AFFORDABLE

4

KNOW WHAT YOU WANT TO SPEND

Once you have a chosen a lender and a loan type you qualify for, your lender will provide a pre-approval or pre-qualification letter. This document is often requested by sellers when putting in an offer to verify the buyer is serious. Also, the majority of real estate agents now request this document before showing any properties. There are a few reasons an agent would want to see this letter.

Unfortunately, we live in a world where real estate agents must protect themselves from dangerous people who wish them harm. Asking to see a pre-qualification letter is one way an agent can filter out those seeking to simply get an individual alone in an empty house with malicious intentions. Seeing this letter also filters out those people who have no intention of buying a home, but just want to see in their neighbor's house (it happens!). Finally, and most importantly the pre-qualification gives you and your agent an idea of how much you can spend on your dream home.

The thing to remember about a pre-approval/pre-qualification is that the lender is only looking at numbers, which do not always tell the whole story. I have seen it happen time and again, a client receives a letter saying they qualify for a loan up to $350,000, so they assume that is their maximum budget. After finding a home for $349,000 that they love, they call their lender and realize that the payments for that loan are way more than they want to spend, OH NO! This why you must discuss with your lender the difference between approval and affordable.

After receiving approval, but before looking at homes, you should always have a candid discussion regarding how much you truly want to pay on a mortgage each month. Just because you can afford something does not automatically make it affordable. If you currently pay rent of $1500 a month and know that you are on a tight budget, you likely will not want a loan with payments higher than your current rent. This is why you should determine upfront what amount you feel comfortable paying each month and convey that information to your lender. They can work backwards from that amount to determine what the total amount you truly want to spend on a home is.

5

HIRE A REALTOR

If you have not already spoken to a real estate agent, now is the time. Most home buyers do not realize how important having their own agent can be in this process. Prior to the early 1990s, agents only represented sellers in real estate transactions. This is where the term, "Buyers Beware," came from, meaning if you are buying a home, watch your back because no one else is! Thankfully, around the mid-90s, states started passing statutes to allow for Buyer's Agency, and by the end of the decade, it became more commonplace.

Today, the majority of buyers see the value in having their own representation and hire a buyer's agent. This is done by signing what is called a Buyer Representation Agreement. This allows the agent to represent the buyer by showing them properties, writing offers, negotiating terms, etc. Real estate agents are trained to know what contracts are needed when and how to best negotiate the terms of any deal. They also should be familiar with the market and be able to tell you what a fair price on any given property is at any given time. Often times, agents also have access to properties not yet listed on online sites that consumers typically search. Basically, they are there to hold your hand through the entire process and make sure you get the right home for your family at the best price.

What many people do not realize is that the Buyer's Agent's commission is paid by the seller. Yes, you read that correctly, you can have your own representation at no additional cost. In Tennessee, almost all listing agreements signed by sellers include a commission set aside to be paid to the buyer's agent at closing. There is no standard amount, but it typically ranges from 2-5% of the sales price. So the only out-of-pocket expense paid by the buyer is a small administrative fee the majority of brokerages charge all clients to keep their information safe and private for 7 years after the transaction. This amount ranges from 0-$750 depending on the agent.

So if you are like most consumers, hiring an agent to represent your interests is a no-brainer. The question is, who do you hire? Throw a rock in Nashville these days and you will hit a real estate agent. Did you know 80% of REALTORS do not make it past their first year in the business? This means, unfortunately, the market is saturated with new agents who statistically will not make it past year one. So before you pick a name off the internet or give cousin Joe your business, it is important you ask a few questions first to determine who will best represent you.

Some agents work for a team while others are independent and own their own business. Team agents typically only represent either buyers or sellers while independent agents do both. One is not better than the other, it is simply a matter of preference you may want to ask about. Due to the pace Nashville is growing, many agents get into the business part-time while still working another full-time job, this is something else you will want to know. Here are a few more questions to use when interviewing agents:

What hours are you available?
Do you prefer to communicate via text, email, phone call, etc
What areas are you comfortable showing homes in?
Do you have a list of trusted vendors you partner with?
Is real estate your primary profession?
Will you be my primary point of contact throughout the transaction?
How many clients do you work with at any given time?
Do you charge an administrative fee?

Do you have experience with new construction?

On average, how many properties do your clients see before making an offer?

Do you work with buyers and sellers?

Do you want to work with me?

This is just an example of a few questions, you probably have some of your own. I have heard horror stories from so many clients who signed with an agent and later realized, they do not work after 5pm or can only show houses on Saturdays, etc. That is why asking for this information upfront is so important.

The key is to feel comfortable with whomever you hire. This person is going to be working for you, and if you do not feel they understand you and your goals, the outcome will most likely not be great. It is imperative you are on the same page upfront so you do not waste time with someone who you do not see eye to eye with and possibly miss out on your dream home because of it.

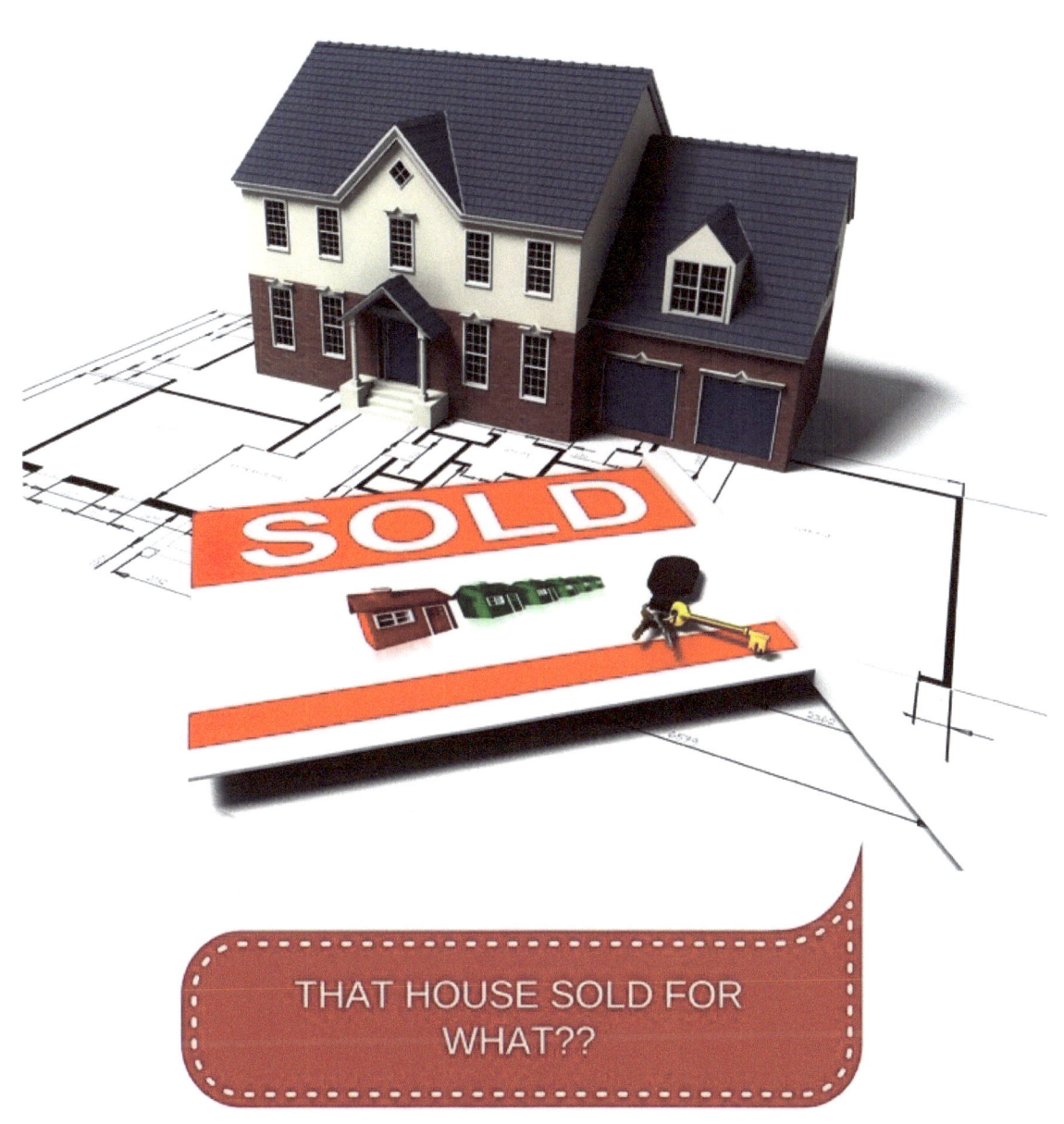

THAT HOUSE SOLD FOR
WHAT??

6

LEARN THE MARKET

When you hire a real estate agent, you are hiring a market expert. Your agent should be able to explain in detail current market statistics for the area you are interested in. You will want to sit down and discuss where you are thinking a good location for your family is and why. Setting realistic expectations is very important before you start viewing houses. For example, if you say you want a 3-bedroom house on half an acre in Brentwood for under $200,000, your agent can tell you that you probably have a better chance of winning the Powerball.

If you are new to the Nashville housing market, you may not know that currently, inventory is low across the board. This means we have what's called a seller's market. In a seller's market, the homeowners who decide to sell are receiving full list price or close to it 9 times out of 10. It also means that houses are not sitting on the market for very long once they are listed, especially in the sub $200,000 price range.

Lots of new construction is being built across Middle Tennessee, but it will take some time for the inventory to catch up to the needs we have in this area. It is currently estimated that Davidson County alone will need just over 19,000 homes by 2022 to keep up with the population growth. So although we are building, it will be a while before the market actually levels out and we have enough homes for all the homebuyers who want to live here.

It is important you understand the market in the area you want to live in so that you are looking at houses in your price range. There is no worse feeling than when a client falls in love with a property and only after realizes it is out of their price range. Make sure this is a conversation you have with your agent. I typically do not show houses to my clients unless I know they are within their budget, but some buyers may still want to see them. Your perfect house may be listed for $2500 more than your budget, so tell your agent if you still want to see homes higher than your budget within a specific range. The key here is to be transparent about where you want to be and how much you are willing to spend to get there. It is up to your agent to tell you if the market will allow for what you want or not. The last thing you want is to waste time looking for something that does not exist.

What Really Matters?

7

PRIORITIZE YOUR WANTS VS. YOUR NEEDS

There is no such thing as the perfect house. There is, however, a perfect house for you, and it is the agent's job to find it. My clients on average see 3-5 houses before making an offer. A lot of buyers come into my office thinking they need to see 20 houses before knowing they found the right one. In the current market, this is just not realistic. Inventory is low so unless your only needs/wants are 4 walls and a roof then we are not going to find that many properties to fit your needs.

Before you look at any properties, you should have a very honest meeting with your agent to discuss your wants vs. your needs. For example, you may want a two-car garage but, you would be okay with a one-car or none at all. On the flip side, there are always a few items on your list that are needs, like two bathrooms opposed to one, or a specific school system. It is important to differentiate between these, so your agent can narrow down available listings as much as possible. No need to waste time looking at houses that you know would never work just because they are in your price range.

I remember my own first-time home buying experience. My husband and I were not super picky, but we did have one requirement: a driveway that fits two cars side by side. This may not seem like much, but to us it was huge! With the hours we worked, if we had to park in a one-lane driveway, we would be blocking each other every single day. So, for the sake of our marriage, a double driveway was key, and we explained that to our agent. For some reason, she kept taking us to properties with single driveways and finally we got to the point where we said no more! We knew we would not buy a house with that feature and it was a waste to even look at them.

So, take some time and really think about what you must have and let your agent know how important these items are for you. You may not have any "must" items and that is okay, being flexible is fantastic. Often with first time buyers especially, you may need to see a few houses before recognizing the features you like and do not like. With my clients, after every house we view, we do a "things I love" and "things I don't love" list so I can help narrow down what really matters most. You may be surprised to find that the things you started out feeling were most important turn out to be not such a big deal in the end.

8

WHEN SEARCHING FOR THE RIGHT PLACE, THINK LONG TERM

Considering your future needs is just as important as your current needs. Ask any homeowner, they will tell you owning a home is expensive. Maintenance is an expense that can sneak up on you if you are not prepared. If you have only ever rented in the past, you may not consider the costs of lawn maintenance or what happens when your HVAC system goes out. On top of your wants and needs, you should consider the future costs of owning a specific property.

Think about the location, is traffic going to get worse or better over the years? Is this the school system I want my children to be in one day? Is the commute to work realistic or too far? Am I too close to my mother-in-law??? These are the kinds of things you want to decide before making any offers.

Consider the home's age and condition. Are you a handyman or know one who will work for free? If not, fixing even small items can add up if you are not prepared. The key is to look at your future and make sure this home lines up with what you want several years from now, not just today. For the 20 years prior to 2008, the National Association of Realtors (NAR) estimated most homeowners stayed in their homes an average of six years. However, in the last ten years, this number has almost doubled. In 2017, NAR reports that the average homeowner stays in their home ten years.

Of course, no one knows what the future holds, but if you are planning a family in a few years, you may not want a two-bedroom, one-bath condo. If you plan to add on to your purchase, be sure to consider codes and sewage lines, will they support your plans? I have seen financial planners estimate the cost of maintaining a home at about 1-2% of the home's value annually. So, in the Nashville area, you are probably looking at anywhere from $2500-$7500 annually in maintenance depending on your home's value. If you do not feel this is something you can prepare for, new construction may be a better option for you, since they often come with warranties and no need to add updates for years to come.

Is this a good investment for my future?

9

CONSIDERING RESALE VALUE

Unless you are one of the very few people who are buying a home with the intention of never moving again, resale value matters. Remember just because you fall in love with a home and it is your perfect place that does not automatically make it valuable when it comes to reselling it one day. There are several things to consider when determining if a home will have a good resale value, the first and most important is location.

You have heard it a million times, "location, location, location"! Where a home is located can be either one of the biggest assets or biggest liabilities. You must consider not only the lot itself, but also where the lot is located. When it comes to the lot, consider the size (can you reach out and touch your neighbor) as well as terrain (is your yard more vertical than horizontal). I have seen houses that require climbing equipment to walk up the driveway; these are never an easy sell. Along with the lot's size and terrain, is it in a location that is good or improving? Many times, homes located on a main road struggle to find buyers who want to deal with the traffic and noise. Walkability is another factor that is becoming more relevant every day. You can use the website, walkscore.com, to determine your location's rating on its walkability. Keep in mind things like a lake view are almost always going to be valued higher than no view. So really look at where the home is and how that area is expected to change when considering resale value. Your agent should be able to help you with determining future value based on location as well.

Size and layout are two more big factors to consider regarding resale. Three bedrooms are almost always going to be valued higher than a two-bedroom regardless of square footage. The same is true of bathrooms; the majority of all buyers will pay more for two baths over one. Even more important is having a master bath of some sort. Even if adding a bath is possible, buyers will typically pay even more than the cost to add one themselves to buy a house that already has one. Open floor plans are still very popular as well as one-level living, or at least the master downstairs. A garage is always going to add a great value to your home, even if it is just for storage. Also keep in mind bigger does not always mean better. Upkeep and maintenance of a large home is not for everyone.

Upgrades can absolutely add value to a home, but only if they are consistent with similar homes in the area. As nice as it sounds, you never want to own the nicest home in the neighborhood. If you spend all your money on lavish upgrades, you may be in for a rude awakening when it comes time to sell. People will not pay twice as much for a home because you had to have that wine cooler and marble counter tops if they can get one similar for less money. Some updates do add value, the key is not to go overboard and stay consistent with market values of the homes in your area.

Negative events are another factor less common but important to consider. If the home you want was involved in a crime, had mold damage, or previously burned down, that can play a role in your resale. Just because you do not mind living in a house someone died in, does not mean the next buyer will feel the same. So before making an offer, look at all these factors to make sure the home will hold or increase its value over time.

10

BE READY TO MAKE AN OFFER

You have found your dream home, now what? The current market in Middle Tennessee is moving very quickly. Homes typically do not sit on the market very long and frequently sellers are receiving multiple offers within days of placing it on the market. Since it is such a hot market, when you fall in love with a home, you need to be ready to move on it. The days of "let me sleep on it" are long gone for this area. So, when you start to view homes, it is vital you are prepared to make an offer.

Assuming you have already contacted a lender and received a pre-approval, the best way to prepare yourself is to be familiar with what is included in a Purchase and Sale Agreement (offer). There are a few key factors included in all offers to familiarize yourself with. Knowing this information upfront could be the difference in your offering coming in before another buyer's offer who was not prepared.

First, you should be prepared to put down a deposit also known as earnest money. Although it is not technically required by law in Tennessee, it is standard practice. Earnest money normally runs anywhere from $500 to 1% of the home's sales price. These funds need to be available as soon as your offer is accepted for immediate deposit. The money will be applied to your purchase, assuming everything runs smoothly and the closing happens as planned. This money protects the seller and shows you are a serious buyer. If you decide you no longer want to buy the home for no good reason, you lose your earnest money. Of course, if the seller backs out for no good reason, you are entitled to a full refund of your money.

The next thing to discuss with your agent is what comes with the home. Many buyers are unaware of which items stay and those that go with the seller. Typically, anything permanently attached stays; this includes bathroom mirrors, lighting fixtures, drapes/blinds and most appliances. Refrigerator and washer/dryer are two examples of appliances that **do not** automatically stay with the home. To be safe, I tell all my clients, if you want to make sure it stays, write it in the contract. On the flip side, if you want to make sure they take their old appliances that also should be spelled out in the contract. The key here is to be specific. If you write the refrigerator stays, you may get whatever refrigerator the seller wants to give you. Instead use specific terms, for example: LG model XYZ stainless steel refrigerator remains. This protects you from any uncertainty in what you are actually coming home to after closing.

Closing date is another item you should consider that will be required. On average, 30-45 days is the amount needed for a lender to close a loan. You need to have this conversation with your lender prior to making an offer. Find out how much time they need and give yourself a little buffer for good measure. Along with date, who will be closing for you? Do you have an attorney to handle the closing or do you want to use a title company? I work with an amazing local title company who the majority of my clients use, but other options are available, if needed.

Other decisions include warranties and inspections. Warranty is something you may want to request if the home is older. A home inspection is a very important part of the home-buying process, but it is not required. If, for example, you are purchasing new construction, you may decide to waive the inspection. In some instances, the seller tells you upfront that they are selling the home "as-is," which means you may get an inspection but they will not fix any items found on it.

The final thing to include is contingencies or special stipulations. For example, if you need to sell your current home before closing on the new one that is something you will need to include in the contract. You may need to include a contingency for your seller as well. Some sellers have listed their home but not yet found a new home to move to. In this case, they ask for a contingency stating they can only close if they have found a new home of their own. Contingencies protect you in many cases, but they also can be a negotiating tool if used properly.

11

MAKE YOUR OFFER THE BEST OFFER

If you have not already heard, an average of 100 people move to the Nashville area every day. Chances are, if you are looking at a property, you are not the only one. It has become commonplace for properties to receive multiple offers, making it a competition among buyers. I have seen homes receive over 20 offers in 48 hours. When a listing agent receives that many offers, they look at a lot more than just the sales price. Agents are getting more and more creative every day in what they offer, so consider a few options that may help give you that edge.

In multiple offer situations, it does not always go to the one who offers the most. In fact, agents must be very careful when reviewing offers much higher than asking price because they may not appraise, which can cause bigger problems down the line. So, first thing you want to do is give the highest offer based on current market trends without going overboard. A way many agents help buyers to make sure their offer is the highest/best is by doing an "escalation clause."

An escalation clause allows you to show the seller what the max price you would be willing to pay is, if your initial offer is not the highest/best offer the sellers receive. For example, you may offer $200,000 on a home, but you are willing to pay up to $208,000 to purchase the home. This clause states you (the buyer) will pay a specific escalated price over the highest/best offer that is received from another buyer up to a certain amount. This protects you from paying more than you must but gives you the peace of mind knowing you gave your best offer.

Dates are another tactic you may use to entice your sellers. No, I do not mean you should take them to dinner…closing date and occupancy date can make a big difference for some sellers. If you could either close very fast or perhaps you are in no hurry at all, either way, use it to your advantage. Your agent should be in touch with the listing agent and, hopefully, be able to determine what timeline the seller prefers. Occupancy date is another factor that can win out when comparing 2 identical offers. If you do not mind giving the homeowner a few days after closing to move out, sometimes, that is all they need to accept an offer. Be flexible if you can and it may make all the difference.

Cash is king, that will always be true. If you are lucky enough to be able to pay all cash, it will give you a distinct advantage. Since most people are not able to do this, consider the more cash you put down, the more desirable you will appear to sellers. Primarily, they just want to know you can afford their home. If you do not have the cash but are working with a local lender and have pre-approval, that goes a long way towards your creditability as a serious buyer.

Finally, a popular new trend is to write a letter to the seller. I have had sellers make the decision to accept a certain offer based solely off a letter from the buyer. Usually, it is something short explaining why you want to own this particular home and what it would mean to you. A little tugging on the heart strings never hurts. Sometimes, pictures are even included, especially if you have an adorable dog or precious children. When a seller is looking at 15 similar offers, something this simple can make all the difference.

Learn the Basics

12

CONTRACTS 101

Now that you have decided to write an offer, there are a few documents all buyers will be required to sign in the State of Tennessee. Real estate agents in this state generally use the same standard documents called TAR (Tennessee Association of Realtors) forms. The TAR forms you will see in the process of buying are: Exclusive Buyer's Representation Agreement, Confirmation of Agency Status, Tennessee Residential Property Condition Disclosure, Disclaimer Notice, and Purchase and Sale Agreement to name a few. Of course, it is always a good idea to read anything before signing it, but here is a little information on these forms so you are better prepared when the time comes.

Exclusive Buyer's Representation Agreement is probably the first document you will see when buying a home. This form is basically a contract between you and your real estate agent of choice. It lays out what type of property you are looking for, where you want to look, and the money you want to spend on it. Also, it will indicate where the agent will search for this property (MLS, for sale by owner, etc.) and list any properties that should be excluded. The Buyer's Agreement will also state the commission your agent will receive for finding you this home (remember that this commission is paid by the seller in 99.99% of all transactions). The document lays out what the agent has agreed to do for you and what you have agreed to do in return. Finally, it tells you that as a real estate agent we are not experts in other fields such as home inspection, land surveying, legal matters, etc. We will refer you for assistance, if needed, to someone who is an expert. This is the paper that hires your agent to represent your best interest throughout the process.

Confirmation of Agency Status is a simple one-page document that certifies who each agent represents in a transaction. This paper is signed first by the home seller and their agent and then by the home buyer and their agent. The document clearly lays out who works for who and in what capacity. This protects unrepresented (not working with an agent) buyers and sellers as well as represented parties.

Tennessee Residential Property Condition Disclosure is a very important document for the buyer to read over. This document is filled out by the seller of the home with no help from the real estate agent. This 5-page form will give you lots of valuable information you will need to consider when making an offer. It tells you how long the current owner has been in the home and any issues they have had while living there. It will also supply you with details about any home owner's association as well as the age of major systems in the home. This document also lists what type of water/sewer supply the home currently has available. It is a wealth of knowledge and should be reviewed in detail. It is signed by the seller when they complete it and then by the buyer once they make an offer.

In some instances, you may receive a Tennessee Residential Property Condition Exemption instead. This document is used if the homeowner has not lived in the home for the last 3 years (it was rented or recently flipped), or if the home was inherited. Also, this document will come into play if it is new construction or basically if for some reason the person selling the home has no information about its condition. When this is the case, the seller is exempt from filling out the full Property Disclosure, because they are likely to not have those details. In these cases, you will need to depend more heavily on your home inspector for this information.

The next document for you to sign will be the Disclaimer Notice. Real estate agents often joke that this is the "agents are dummies" document. The purpose of this form is to remind buyers that real estate agents are not experts in all matters and they should contact an expert for any other questions. Items mentioned include: roofing, home inspection, termites, zoning, flood insurance, septic systems, school districts, etc. The purpose of this form is to remind buyers they should double-check all information on a property for accuracy prior to purchasing it.

The Purchase and Sell Agreement is one of the most important forms a buyer will review. This is essentially your offer to buy a home you want and once signed by all parties becomes a contract between seller and buyer. This document will include your offer price, what items you want left in the home (or removed), financing you will use, earnest money amount, closing date, who will pay for title fees and closing costs, warranty information, inspection information, and any other special stipulations. Your agent will walk through all this with you prior to signing, but it is important to read it all and double check for accuracy. This document lays out contingencies to be met and what the consequences of not meeting them will be. It explains in what instances your earnest money will be refunded in the event the contract falls through and when it will go to the seller instead. Once this form is completed and sent to the seller, they have the option of accepting it, rejecting it, or countering it. If you receive a counter, that will be on a new document that your agent should review with you. Once all terms are agreed upon and both parties have signed and received copies, the contract will be bound by one of the agents and you are officially under contract!

Keep in mind if you decide to go with new construction, the builders will usually have their own paperwork that they use different from the standard TAR forms discussed here. Often, the same information is used but written in a different way and with more detail added regarding the new construction. Keep in mind you will want to have your agent review this document with you in detail prior to signing anything.

POP QUIZ

13

TERMS TO KNOW- A GLOSSARY*

appraisal

    A written justification of the price paid for a property, primarily based on an analysis of comparable sales of similar homes nearby.

appraised value

    An opinion of a property's fair market value, based on an appraiser's knowledge, experience, and analysis of the property. Since an appraisal is based primarily on comparable sales, and the most recent sale is the one on the property in question, the appraisal usually comes out at the purchase price.

chain of title

    An analysis of the transfers of title to a piece of property over the years.

clear title

    A title that is free of liens or legal questions as to ownership of the property.

closing

    This has different meanings in different states. In some states, a real estate transaction is not considered "closed" until the documents record at the local recorder's office. In others, the "closing" is a meeting where all of the documents are signed and money changes hands.

closing costs

    Closing costs are separated into what are called "non-recurring closing costs" and "pre-paid items." Non-recurring closing costs are any items which are paid just once as a result of buying the property or obtaining a loan. "Pre-paids" are items which recur over time, such as property taxes and homeowner's insurance. A lender makes an attempt to estimate the amount of non-recurring closing costs and prepaid items on the Good Faith Estimate which they must issue to the borrower within three days of receiving a home loan application.

cloud on title

Any conditions revealed by a title search that adversely affect the title to real estate. Usually, clouds on title cannot be removed except by deed, release, or court action.

co-borrower

An additional individual who is both obligated on the loan and is on title to the property.

commission

Most salespeople earn commissions for the work that they do and there are many sales professionals involved in each transaction, including Realtors, loan officers, title representatives, attorneys, escrow representative, and representatives for pest companies, home warranty companies, home inspection companies, insurance agents, and more. The commissions are paid out of the charges paid by the seller or buyer in the purchase transaction. Realtors generally earn the largest commissions, followed by lenders, then the others.

common area assessments

In some areas, they are called Homeowners Association Fees. They are charges paid to the Homeowners Association by the owners of the individual units in a condominium or planned unit development (PUD) and are generally used to maintain the property and common areas.

common areas

Those portions of a building, land, and amenities owned (or managed) by a planned unit development (PUD) or condominium project's homeowners' association (or a cooperative project's cooperative corporation) that are used by all of the unit owners, who share in the common expenses of their operation and maintenance. Common areas include swimming pools, tennis courts, and other recreational facilities, as well as common corridors of buildings, parking areas, means of ingress and egress, etc.

comparable sales

Recent sales of similar properties in nearby areas and used to help determine the market value of a property. Also referred to as "comps."

contingency

A condition that must be met before a contract is legally binding. For example, home purchasers often include a contingency that specifies that the contract is not binding until the purchaser obtains a satisfactory home inspection report from a qualified home inspector.

contract

An oral or written agreement to do or not to do a certain thing.

deed

The legal document conveying title to a property.

deposit

A sum of money given in advance of a larger amount being expected in the future. Often called in real estate an "earnest money deposit."

discount points

In the mortgage industry, this term is usually used only in reference to government loans, meaning FHA and VA loans. Discount points refer to any "points" paid in addition to the one percent loan origination fee. A "point" is one percent of the loan amount.

down payment

The part of the purchase price of a property that the buyer pays in cash and does not finance with a mortgage.

earnest money deposit

A deposit made by the potential home buyer to show that he or she is serious about buying the house.

easement

A right of way giving persons other than the owner access to or over a property.

equity

A homeowner's financial interest in a property. Equity is the difference between the fair market value of the property and the amount still owed on its mortgage and other liens.

escrow

An item of value, money, or documents deposited with a third party to be delivered upon the fulfillment of a condition. For example, the earnest money deposit is put into escrow until delivered to the seller when the transaction is closed.

examination of title

The report on the title of a property from the public records or an abstract of the title.

exclusive listing

A written contract that gives a licensed real estate agent the exclusive right to sell a property for a specified time.

fair market value

The highest price that a buyer, willing but not compelled to buy, would pay, and the lowest a seller, willing but not compelled to sell, would accept.

Fannie Mae (FNMA)

The Federal National Mortgage Association, which is a congressionally chartered, shareholder-owned company that is the nation's largest supplier of home mortgage funds.

Federal Housing Administration (FHA)

An agency of the U.S. Department of Housing and Urban Development (HUD). Its main activity is the insuring of residential mortgage loans made by private lenders. The FHA sets standards for construction and underwriting but does not lend money or plan or construct housing.

FHA mortgage

A mortgage that is insured by the Federal Housing Administration (FHA). Along with VA loans, an FHA loan will often be referred to as a government loan.

fiduciary

a person to whom property or power is entrusted for the benefit of another.

firm commitment

A lender's agreement to make a loan to a specific borrower on a specific property.

fixture

Personal property that becomes real property when attached in a permanent manner to real estate.

grantee

A The person to whom an interest in real property is conveyed.

grantor

A The person conveying an interest in real property.

home inspection

A A thorough inspection by a professional that evaluates the structural and mechanical condition of a property. A satisfactory home inspection is often included as a contingency by the purchaser.

homeowners' association

A A nonprofit association that manages the common areas of a planned unit development (PUD) or condominium project. In a condominium project, it has no ownership interest in the common elements. In a PUD project, it holds title to the common elements.

homeowner's insurance

A An insurance policy that combines personal liability insurance and hazard insurance coverage for a dwelling and its contents.

homeowner's warranty

A A type of insurance often purchased by homebuyers that will cover repairs to certain items, such as heating or air conditioning, should they break down within the coverage period. The buyer often requests the seller to pay for this coverage as a condition of the sale, but either party can pay.

lease option

A An alternative financing option that allows home buyers to lease a home with an option to buy. Each month's rent payment may consist of not only the rent, but also an additional amount which can be applied toward the down payment on an already specified price.

legal description

A A property description, recognized by law, that is sufficient to locate and identify the property without oral testimony.

lender

A term which can refer to the institution making the loan or to the individual representing the firm. For example, loan officers are often referred to as "lenders."

liabilities

A person's financial obligations. Liabilities include long-term and short-term debt, as well as any other amounts that are owed to others.

lien

A legal claim against a property that must be paid off when the property is sold. A mortgage or first trust deed is considered a lien.

liquid asset

A cash asset or an asset that is easily converted into cash.

loan

A sum of borrowed money (principal) that is generally repaid with interest.

loan officer

Also referred to by a variety of other terms, such as lender, loan representative, loan "rep," account executive, and others. The loan officer serves several functions and has various responsibilities: they solicit loans, they are the representative of the lending institution, and they represent the borrower to the lending institution.

loan origination

How a lender refers to the process of obtaining new loans.

loan servicing

After you obtain a loan, the company you make the payments to is "servicing" your loan. They process payments, send statements, manage the escrow/impound account, provide collection efforts on delinquent loans, ensure that insurance and property taxes are made on the property, handle pay-offs and assumptions, and provide a variety of other services.

loan-to-value (LTV)

The percentage relationship between the amount of the loan and the appraised value or sales price (whichever is lower).

lock-in

An agreement in which the lender guarantees a specified interest rate for a certain amount of time at a certain cost.

mortgage

A legal document that pledges a property to the lender as security for payment of a debt. Instead of mortgages, some states use First Trust Deeds.

mortgage broker

A mortgage company that originates loans, then places those loans with a variety of other lending institutions with whom they usually have pre-established relationships.

mortgagee

The lender in a mortgage agreement.

mortgage insurance (MI)

Insurance that covers the lender against some of the losses incurred as a result of a default on a home loan. Often mistakenly referred to as PMI, which is actually the name of one of the larger mortgage insurers. Mortgage insurance is usually required in one form or another on all loans that have a loan-to-value higher than eighty percent. Mortgages above 80% LTV that call themselves "No MI" are usually made at a higher interest rate. Instead of the borrower paying the mortgage insurance premiums directly, they pay a higher interest rate to the lender, which then pays the mortgage insurance themselves. Also, FHA loans and certain first-time homebuyer programs require mortgage insurance regardless of the loan-to-value.

mortgage insurance premium (MIP)

The amount paid by a mortgagor for mortgage insurance, either to a government agency such as the Federal Housing Administration (FHA) or to a private mortgage insurance (MI) company.

mortgage life and disability insurance

A type of term life insurance often bought by borrowers. The amount of coverage decreases as the principal balance declines. Some policies also cover the borrower in the event of disability. In the event that the borrower dies while the policy is in force, the debt is automatically satisfied by insurance proceeds.

mortgagor

>The borrower in a mortgage agreement.

note

>A legal document that obligates a borrower to repay a mortgage loan at a stated interest rate during a specified period of time.

original principal balance

>The total amount of principal owed on a mortgage before any payments are made.

origination fee

>On a government loan, the loan origination fee is one percent of the loan amount, but additional points may be charged which are called "discount points." One point equals one percent of the loan amount. On a conventional loan, the loan origination fee refers to the total number of points a borrower pays.

owner financing

>A property purchase transaction in which the property seller provides all or part of the financing.

personal property

>Any property that is not real property.

PITI

>This stands for principal, interest, taxes and insurance. If you have an "impounded" loan, then your monthly payment to the lender includes all of these and probably includes mortgage insurance as well. If you do not have an impounded account, then the lender still calculates this amount and uses it as part of determining your debt-to-income ratio.

planned unit development (PUD)

>A type of ownership where individuals actually own the building or unit they live in, but common areas are owned jointly with the other members of the development or association. Contrast with condominium, where an individual actually owns the airspace of his unit, but the buildings and common areas are owned jointly with the others in the development or association.

point

>A point is 1 percent of the amount of the mortgage.

power of attorney
    A legal document that authorizes another person to act on one's behalf. A power of
    attorney can grant complete authority or can be limited to certain acts and/or certain
    periods of time.
pre-approval
    A loosely used term which is generally taken to mean that a borrower has completed a
    loan application and provided debt, income, and savings documentation which an
    underwriter has reviewed and approved. A pre-approval is usually done at a certain
    loan amount and making assumptions about what the interest rate will actually be at
    the time the loan is actually made, as well as estimates for the amount that will be paid
    for property taxes, insurance and others. A pre-approval applies only to the borrower.
    Once a property is chosen, it must also meet the underwriting guidelines of the lender.
    Contrast with pre-qualification.
pre-qualification
    This usually refers to the loan officer's written opinion of the ability of a borrower to
    qualify for a home loan, after the loan officer has made inquiries about debt, income,
    and savings. The information provided to the loan officer may have been presented
    verbally or in the form of documentation, and the loan officer may or may not have
    reviewed a credit report on the borrower.
prime rate
    The interest rate that banks charge to their preferred customers. Changes in the prime
    rate are widely publicized in the news media and are used as the indexes in some
    adjustable rate mortgages, especially home equity lines of credit. Changes in the prime
    rate do not directly affect other types of mortgages, but the same factors that
    influence the prime rate also affect the interest rates of mortgage loans.
principal
    The amount borrowed or remaining unpaid. The part of the monthly payment that
    reduces the remaining balance of a mortgage.
principal balance
    The outstanding balance of principal on a mortgage. The principal balance does not
    include interest or any other charges.

principal, interest, taxes, and insurance (PITI)

> The four components of a monthly mortgage payment on impounded loans. Principal refers to the part of the monthly payment that reduces the remaining balance of the mortgage. Interest is the fee charged for borrowing money. Taxes and insurance refer to the amounts that are paid into an escrow account each month for property taxes and mortgage and hazard insurance.

private mortgage insurance (MI)

> Mortgage insurance that is provided by a private mortgage insurance company to protect lenders against loss if a borrower defaults. Most lenders generally require MI for a loan with a loan-to-value (LTV) percentage in excess of 80 percent.

promissory note

> A written promise to repay a specified amount over a specified period of time.

purchase agreement

> A written contract signed by the buyer and seller stating the terms and conditions under which a property will be sold.

rate lock

> A commitment issued by a lender to a borrower or other mortgage originator guaranteeing a specified interest rate for a specified period of time at a specific cost.

real estate agent

> A person licensed to negotiate and transact the sale of real estate.

Real Estate Settlement Procedures Act (RESPA)

> A consumer protection law that requires lenders to give borrowers advance notice of closing costs.

real property

> Land and appurtenances, including anything of a permanent nature such as structures, trees, minerals, and the interest, benefits, and inherent rights thereof.

recorder

> The public official who keeps records of transactions that affect real property in the area. Sometimes known as a "Registrar of Deeds" or "County Clerk."

recording
> The noting in the registrar's office of the details of a properly executed legal document, such as a deed, a mortgage note, a satisfaction of mortgage, or an extension of mortgage, thereby making it a part of the public record.

revolving debt
> A credit arrangement, such as a credit card, that allows a customer to borrow against a preapproved line of credit when purchasing goods and services. The borrower is billed for the amount that is actually borrowed plus any interest due.

right of first refusal
> A provision in an agreement that requires the owner of a property to give another party the first opportunity to purchase or lease the property before he or she offers it for sale or lease to others.

right of ingress or egress
> The right to enter or leave designated premises.

sale-leaseback
> A technique in which a seller deeds property to a buyer for a consideration, and the buyer simultaneously leases the property back to the seller.

second mortgage
> A mortgage that has a lien position subordinate to the first mortgage.

secondary market
> The buying and selling of existing mortgages, usually as part of a "pool" of mortgages.

secured loan
> A loan that is backed by collateral.

security
> The property that will be pledged as collateral for a loan.

subdivision
> A housing development that is created by dividing a tract of land into individual lots for sale or lease.

survey
> A drawing or map showing the precise legal boundaries of a property, the location of improvements, easements, rights of way, encroachments, and other physical features.

third-party origination

> A process by which a lender uses another party to completely or partially originate, process, underwrite, close, fund, or package the mortgages it plans to deliver to the secondary mortgage market.

title

> A legal document evidencing a person's right to or ownership of a property.

title company

> A company that specializes in examining and insuring titles to real estate.

title insurance

> Insurance that protects the lender (lender's policy) or the buyer (owner's policy) against loss arising from disputes over ownership of a property.

title search

> A check of the title records to ensure that the seller is the legal owner of the property and that there are no liens or other claims outstanding.

transfer of ownership

> Any means by which the ownership of a property changes hands. Lenders consider all of the following situations to be a transfer of ownership: the purchase of a property "subject to" the mortgage, the assumption of the mortgage debt by the property purchaser, and any exchange of possession of the property under a land sales contract or any other land trust device.

transfer tax

> State or local tax payable when title passes from one owner to another.

Truth-in-Lending

> A federal law that requires lenders to fully disclose, in writing, the terms and conditions of a mortgage, including the annual percentage rate (APR) and other charges.

trustee

> A fiduciary who holds or controls property for the benefit of another.

*All glossary terms provided by: N. (2018) *Real Estate & Mortgage Resources.* Accessed February 16, 2018 through https://www.realestateabc.com/glossary/index.htm

Your Money:

A TIMELINE

14

WHEN DO I PAY FOR THAT?

You know you will have to pay closing costs and a down payment to purchase your home. What you may not know is that all that money is not just due at the closing table, some is due before you close. No one wants to be surprised when it comes to money being owed, here is a general guideline so you know what to expect.

TIMELINE:
-Offer Accepted, you are officially under contract!

-**Earnest Money** is due typically within 3-5 days of binding a contract. That amount is usually anywhere from a flat $500 to 1% of the purchase price and needs to be immediately available funds (no credit cards). This money will be deposited as soon as it is received into an escrow account and held there till closing. At closing time, the money will be applied towards your closing costs.

-**Home Inspection** is the next expense you will need to be prepared to pay. In almost all situations, you will want to order a home inspection as soon as you go under contract. In the event the inspector finds an issue it is better to know sooner than later. A typical home inspection runs anywhere from $275-$500 just depending on the size of the home (the bigger the home, the more expensive the inspection). It is due at the time of the inspection, and in most instances can be paid either cash or credit. But always talk with your lender before putting any charges on your credit card while in the process of applying for a loan.

-Termite Inspection is usually done close to the same time as the home inspection, and in some instances can be scheduled together. This inspection usually runs between $50-$75 and is paid at the time it is completed. Some companies will allow you to pay for the inspection at closing, but it is more common to pay for it when it occurs in case the home does not close for any reason.

-Appraisal is usually ordered within 2 weeks of going under contract by your lender. This is another item that you will need to pay for upfront just in case the loan does not close as expected. The appraisal fee is typically between $400-$500 and is not something you can shop around for, because it is ordered by your lender. The only time an appraisal is not required is when you pay cash for the property and waive the appraisal contingency.

-Remaining Closing Costs will all be paid at the closing table in one lump sum. You will receive a Closing Disclosure at least 3 days prior to your closing so you can review and approve the final cost to close. Things such as taxes, insurance, origination fee, etc. will be included in this sum. You will bring this amount, including down payment, with you to the closing table in the form of a certified check or money order. You can also have the funds wired directly from your bank if you wish.

This is a good estimate of your timeline to close and what you will owe, but remember to always check with your lender and/or Realtor® if you have any questions regarding upfront costs.

Is it Worth it
To Warranty it?

15

HOME WARRANTY OR NOT?

Home warranties can be a huge money saver for home owners in the first few years of home ownership, especially. According to 2-10 Home Buyers Warranty, homeowners have a 68% chance of a system or appliance failing in their first year of homeownership. Also 1 in 2.1 homes experience an HVAC repair. A furnace repair can run about $3800, and if you are like most new homeowners, it would be very hard to come up with that amount of cash in a hurry. This is why home warranties have become so popular for new home owners.

A typical home warranty will run anywhere from $400-$600 dollars annually. The warranty is something that can be purchased by the home seller to entice buyers or by the buyer themselves. Also, warranties are sometimes offered by the listing agent to new homeowners. This is done quite often if it is known that the home systems are older and will most likely need to be repaired in the near future. This takes some of the fear away from homebuyers since they can fall back on their warranty if something breaks soon after closing.

A home warranty is like home insurance, but it covers what most home insurance policies will not, such as HVAC systems, plumbing, appliances, and electrical. You can also add coverage for things like roofs, pools, and septic tanks. Similar to insurance, you pay for it whether you use it or not, but in the event you need it you will be very happy to have it. Basically, if you have an issue with a covered system you call the warranty company and they send a local technician to repair or replace it for a service fee. Service fees are typically $75-150 and are similar to paying your deductible on an insurance policy.

If you are aware that the appliances and our major home systems are out of date, a home warranty is always a good idea. You can continue to renew your home warranty even after your first year of home ownership, so your coverage continues. It is a nice piece of mind to have as a home owner and I recommend it to all my clients buying a home more than 10 years old that has not been updated.

NO HOME IS PERFECT

16

HOME INSPECTIONS

I am lucky enough to be married to a licensed home inspector. My husband has given me a special insider's perspective into the importance of a good inspection. I would very seldom, if ever, recommend purchasing a home without having it inspected first. Even new construction homes are often inspected before closing as a precaution. It is amazing how something small can turn into a major repair if left unnoticed. Regardless of how much you think you know about homes, a home inspector most likely knows more and will give an objective report of all issues.

When choosing a home inspector, cheapest is not always the best. You want to work with someone who is licensed and experienced in the Middle Tennessee area. Your real estate agent will no doubt have a few to recommend based on past experiences with them. Trust me when I say not all inspectors are created equal. Typically, you can expect to pay somewhere between $300-$400 for an average-sized home (2200 square feet) in Nashville. This is money well spent for the peace of mind you will have moving forward.

The inspection is the first thing you want accomplished after going under contract. If there are any major issues that need addressed, it is best to know sooner than later. Your agent will most likely schedule the inspection for you. It is not necessary for you to attend the inspection, but you can do so if you would like. Personally, I like to attend all inspections for my buyers, so they do not have to, but again it is your call. The inspection will take anywhere from 3-4 hours and it is important you allow the professional to do their job. So, if you plan to attend, it is recommended you show up at the end so the inspector can finish up and then walk through and show you any issues he/she found.

If you want to be present for the entire inspection, that is ok, but try not to follow the inspector around and ask questions about everything. They are professionals and will explain everything to you in their report, but they are more likely to miss something if you are constantly interrupting their process. Feel free to use this time to take measurements, look at design options, and plan your furniture placings. Something else important to note, you should never attempt to follow an inspector or any professional up a ladder (to the roof/attic) or into a crawl space. They are trained professionals and will take plenty of photos for you, there is no need to endanger yourself or others just to get a closer look.

The inspector will look at most major systems, roofs, electrical, foundation, etc. Keep in mind they are there to tell you if something does not look like it should or is not functioning properly. It is not the inspector's job to tell you how something should be fixed or what it might cost. For example, they may tell you the A/C is not functioning properly, but you should call an HVAC expert for specific problems and repair estimates.

Many buyers often ask inspectors, what should I ask to be fixed? This is not a question your inspector can answer. Once you receive your inspection report and review it, you should call your real estate agent to discuss your options. Everyone has a different idea of what is considered acceptable when buying home. I have had some buyers who are handy and know they can handle most issues themselves, once they are aware of them. On the other hand, other buyers want to move into a house with as little imperfections as possible and want every little thing corrected. This is a discussion to have with your agent after the inspection is completed.

No home is in such great shape that a report will come back clean. All homes whether they are 70 years old or 7 will have items that are in need of fixing or replacing. It is up to you and your agent to discuss what you are and are not willing to handle yourself versus asking the seller to fix before closing. Several factors will need to be considered when determining what to ask for. For example, if you are in a lower price point with several buyers competing with multiple offers, you may not want to ask for as much since the seller could just say no and fall back on a backup offer. If you feel the home was overpriced a bit, you may find yourself asking for more to give you the value you expect at that price. Also, in new construction or on a flip home, buyers will typically want things to be in better shape since the work is being done by a licensed contractor with a warranty in place.

Keep in mind you always have the option of asking the seller to reduce the price or pay some closing costs in lieu of repairs. At times, it is easier for a seller to give you money out of their closing than it is to pay out of pocket beforehand for repairs. Another thing to remember is that if your inspection comes back with something major (serious foundation issues, mold, etc.) you can choose to walk away, and your earnest money will be refunded in full. On the flip side, it is not unheard of to ask for nothing. Do not feel you have to nit-pick or ask for repairs that are minor just to ask for something.

Once you have decided what you want repaired/replaced, your agent will write up a repair proposal for the seller's agent to review with the homeowner. The two agents will then have a specified amount of time (timeframe is detailed in your contract, typically a few days) to negotiate on behalf of their clients and come to an agreement. Once an agreement is met, a repair amendment will be signed by both the buyer and seller stating when the buyer will re-inspect to verify repairs have been made. You can also choose to ask for receipts/warranty info in lieu of or along with a re-inspection. It is a good idea to not wait till the day before closing to reinspect repairs and make sure work is complete. In reality, if the work is not done and you are about to close most people end up closing anyways because they do not want to delay their move. I usually ask repairs are completed within 2 weeks of the repair amendment so there is plenty of time to verify the work is complete before closing.

Here are a few of the most common issues reported by inspectors in the Nashville area:

Kitchen range is missing anti-tip device- easy repair but important safety issue especially if you have small children;

Gutter downspout discharge is too close to foundation- another easy fix, should be repaired to alleviate erosion and water seeping below foundation;

GFCI (ground fault circuit interrupter) not being installed where it is required, such as kitchen/bathroom/exterior/garage outlets- commonly done by licensed electrician and required on new homes to meet code regulations.

Doors and windows not functioning properly (locking/closing) is another common deficiency found by inspectors and something a handyman can easily repair in most instances.

These are just a few examples of items you will most likely see on your inspection. Keep in mind if you ever have questions or do not understand something on the report your inspector is always happy to answer your questions. Inspectors want to help you understand you home systems and how to care for them properly, all you have to do is ask.

what's it really worth?

17

APPRAISALS: THE GOOD, THE BAD, AND THE UGLY

If you are taking out a loan to purchase your home, you will be required to have your home appraised. An appraisal is done to determine the home's fair market value. This value is determined primarily by comparing recently sold properties in the vicinity that are comparable to the home being appraised. The appraiser uses the most recently sold homes that have similar features and are in a close radius. As a home buyer, you want the home to be valued at the sales price or higher. Problems can arise with your loan if the home does not appraise for at least the sales price. But it does not have to be a deal breaker, there are options if the home does not appraise.

Of course, you want to do everything you can to make sure you are not overpaying for a home. This is one of the reasons having a good agent is so important as a buyer. Your agent should be comparing the property you want to other recent sales in the area to determine what the fair market value is before you even look at it. This can be a task in the Nashville market because of the low inventory. Many homes are receiving multiple offers. In multiple offer situations, many buyers start offering higher and higher amounts, which can drive the price up higher than it will ever appraise for. Even though your agent knows what the fair market value should be, they may recommend offering more due to the competition with other buyers. So, although you want to make the best offer, always consider if you go too high you are more likely to get in trouble when it comes time to get it appraised.

Appraisals are ordered by the lender and are done anonymously through an appraisal company, so the lender does not have contact with the actual appraiser. It is done this way, so the appraiser will be completely objective when determining value. Once ordered, the appraiser will come out to the home and take photos and measurements to evaluate the fair market value. They take square footage, how many bathrooms/bedrooms, upgrades, yard size, and materials all into account when looking for similar homes. They use predetermined equations to equal out homes that are similar but not identical. If there are no similar homes in the area, they will go a little further out to find something comparable.

If you receive your appraisal back and it is lower than expected, you have a few options. Unfortunately, a lender will not write a loan for more than the appraised amount, so this means the buyer either has to bring more money to closing or the seller has to drop the price. Another option is to have buyer and seller meet in the middle. So, if the buyer is under contract on a home at $200,000 and the home appraises at $190,000 then the seller could drop the price $5,000 and the buyer can bring $5,000 more to closing. If possible, this is a nice option to make both parties happy.

This is not always possible for buyers who may not have the extra cash. Normally the buyer's and seller's agents will work together to do everything they can to make a deal work when a home does not appraise. It is possible to send an appraiser comps you have found that are in line with your sales price if it comes back low and you feel it is wrong. They may or may not revisit the appraised price, but in most instances, they will stick to their guns. So the thing to remember is, try and keep your offer in line with similar sales in the area, and if you go over, be ready for the chance you will need extra money at closing. The good news is that once the home does come back and the appraisal is good that means you are almost ready to close. The appraisal is the last hurdle before the finish line!

18

STAY CALM WHEN THINGS COME UP

One of the main reasons I became a real estate agent was to help people have fun buying their dream home. Working in the mortgage industry and then in insurance, I saw how stressed home buyers were throughout the transaction and thought there has to be a better way. Then as a first-time buyer, I felt the stress myself. As it turns out much of that stress stems from a lack of communication between the agent and the client and/or the lender. Unfortunately, as with any other profession, not all Realtors® are created equal. Some agents only do real estate on the side and have other careers that take up most of their time. Other agents simply are not blessed with the ability to easily explain and handle problems as they arise. Being available and able to effectively communicate are two very important factors to consider before hiring your agent.

I mention these important qualities to consider because it is inevitable that at some point during your transaction something will go wrong. I have yet to see a buyer go from offer to closing without something arising that was initially unforeseen. Typically, this is when the stress arrives making your stomach churn and your head hurt. The best thing you can do is relax and trust your agent. In most cases, whatever has occurred has happened before and we will know what to do. There is always a solution you just have to give your trusted partners (whether it be your lender or your agent) time to find the answer and solve the issue.

This is why I ask my clients to text me when they feel anxious. Buying a home is one of the biggest financial decisions you will ever make. Naturally, even the most prepared buyers will feel anxiety, that is normal. But, if you trust the people you are working with then it makes everything run so much smoother. So, when your inspector tells you the home has termites, or your appraisal comes back low, take a breath and know it will be okay.

I am a firm believer in if it is meant to happen it will. I say this to every client at least once or twice without fail. Sometimes, we may not know why, but the home you thought was your dream home (but your offer didn't get accepted) turns out to be nothing compared to the perfect home you find 2 weeks later and close on. I see it all the time, things often work out as they should. So, my most important piece of advice is to KEEP CALM AND TRUST YOUR REALTOR.

congratulations!

19

CLOSING DAY

Closing day is exciting and fairly simple if you are prepared. Three days prior to your closing, you should have received a closing disclosure (CD) detailing all the money you will be paying and what it is going towards. It includes loan details such as estimated monthly payment including taxes and insurance. It is extremely important you review this document and understand all the figures. Your lender will be happy to answer any questions you may have so you feel good about it. Keep in mind, you get this document early so that there are no surprises at closing, and if you find an error you still have time to correct it.

Do not be surprised if something needs corrected, with all the moving parts of a home loan it is common to find an error somewhere. For example, one of my clients was preparing to close and suddenly the payment was higher than we had expected. After looking at the CD, we realized the title company had accidently charged taxes for two years instead of one year. All it took to fix was an email to the title company and they sent us a corrected CD. This is the reason we want to review these documents early, so you are not surprised by anything at closing.

In the week prior to your closing, you should be reaching out to the local utility companies to set your services up. Most companies can do this online or over the phone, but in some rural areas you may have to visit the local office to get things set up. You will want to get everything put into your name effective the closing date. This includes: electricity, water/sewer, gas (if applicable), cable, phone lines, internet and any security system you may have set up. Your agent should have a list of contacts and/or preferred vendors who can help you accomplish these tasks. You also should have already spoken with an insurance agent regarding home insurance. If you have not, make sure you complete this task the week before closing. Remember bundling your new home policy with an existing auto policy is always a savings as well as going with a higher deductible.

By the time you arrive at the closing table, you should have completed your final walkthrough as well. I recommend doing a final walkthrough the morning before closing or the night before; the closer to closing, the better. (Keep in mind the final walkthrough is not the same as the re-inspection you may want to do if you have asked for repairs.) As a home buyer, you want to make sure your new home looks the same or better than it was last time you saw it. If you show up and a tree limb has fallen on the roof in a storm the night before closing, that is something you would want to be aware of (it has happened!). You may even decide to postpone your closing if you are not satisfied with the home's condition, and it is your right to do so. Most of the time, everything goes smoothly, but you never want to assume this is the case, ALWAYS do a walkthrough before closing and sign off that everything looks good.

After you have reviewed your closing disclosure and you have completed your walkthrough, your next step is to get a cashier's check for the amount you need to close. You also have the option of your bank wiring the funds directly to the buyer; this is normally done when the amount is over $10,000. However you send it, double check you have the correct amount before doing anything. Along with your money to close, you will also need to have your driver's license available at closing to have copied for the records. Finally, bring your favorite blue pen and be ready to start signing.

Typically, the actual closing process only takes about 30 minutes to one hour. It is not uncommon for you to close around the same time as the current homeowners, but if not, you may have to wait for them to close before you are given ownership and keys. They, of course, want to make sure funds have been received before they sign their home over. Once both parties have completed closing, you will receive copies of all the paperwork and keys to your new home. This is also when you will receive additional items such as garage door openers or keys to any neighborhood pool, etc. Unless you previously agreed to let the sellers stay in the home for a bit, you can start moving in immediately. It is always a good idea to get the locks changed, even though you should have all the keys it is a good safety precaution to take.

A few other things new home buyers sometimes forget about having readily available are: toilet paper, paper towels, cleaning supplies, paper plates, towels, shower curtains and soap. It is a good idea to have these items in a Tupperware container you can easily find when moving.

Congratulations, you are officially a homeowner! Now, it is time to relax with your family and enjoy your new home.

ABOUT THE AUTHOR

Amy Robinson is a license REALTOR in the state of Tennessee. Amy was raised in Mt. Juliet, Tennessee, which is just outside Nashville. Other than the time she spent in Knoxville earning her degree from The University of Tennessee, Nashville has always been home for Amy. She currently helps buyers find their dream home as the Lead Buyer's Agent for The McKissack Group with Parks Realty. When she is not working with clients, you can find her with her husband at their Mt. Juliet home playing with her 3 dogs, grilling out and having a cocktail. For more information about Amy and how she can help you realize your dream of home ownership, visit her website at: www.parksathome.com/agents/AmyRobinson

www.ingramcontent.com/pod-product-compliance
Lightning Source LLC
Chambersburg PA
CBHW041458280526
45792CB00004B/1047